I Don't Need to Make a Pretty Thing

I Don't Need to Make a Pretty Thing

poems

Michelle S. Reed

Black
Lawrence
Press

www.blacklawrence.com

Executive Editor: Diane Goettel
Book and cover design: Amy Freels

Copyright © 2016 Michelle S. Reed
ISBN: 978-1-62557-959-1

Published 2016 by Black Lawrence Press.
Printed in the United States.

For Perrin, for Ruth, and for Ruby.

Contents

How to Go Home

Think of your mother making coffee
early on Sundays. How she pours
water into the machine carefully,

the folds of her skin blue and soft
in morning light. How she moves
about the house in a slow circle

while the coffee brews, opening
each window to let the breeze in.
How the little dog follows her

like she is some kind of beacon,
both of them stepping in and out
of patches of sun on carpet. How,

in moments of sun, your mother's
bathrobe almost glows. This dance
is a map. This memory a compass.

She is not where you are going
or where you have been.

Catcall #48

I'm in the dairy aisle
when the old man stumbles
toward me. *If an apple*

is falling, he asks,
is the moon also falling?
We are alone

with the creams
and cheeses. I pretend
not to hear him. *Listen,*

he says, *something lives*
in the core of a bullet.
Something

moves there. Something
hums. I fill my cart
with yogurt. *Something*

more than patience.
Something like a snake.
I search for packaged

vegetables, and he stares
at me as if he knows
my name. *I have*

to tell you, he whispers,
the world is not what you
want it to be.

He gestures wildly
at the frozen blueberries.
Every moment

another garden. His lined
hands close around mine.
His eyes are gray

and cold, cold and gray.
A moon in free fall
every hour of every day.

I Tell You Someone I Love is Dead,

and you take me out to lunch.
We eat french fries together
in restaurant light. This is what
we know: the comfort of afternoon
hamburgers, grace of tiny
packets of ketchup, salvation
in filling ourselves with more
than we need. I go home and try
to follow a yoga video. I bend
over my legs and swing
my torso back and forth,
then I rise up slowly
like a monster in one of those movies
I'm too afraid to watch.
*Now shine your heart
forward*, the woman in the video
says, and for a moment,
I think it could be that simple,
to arch the spine a certain way,
to lift the head, to close
the eyes and glow.

Letter for M

I haven't seen a bat here, but every morning
spiders crawl out of my radiator, searching for me.

That is to say, even the creatures in Pennsylvania seem
to follow me, just like the river on black

August evenings, stars unraveling above its silvered belly.
I miss your cats. I wonder how tall your daughter is,

if her eyes are as blue as they were. I wonder if you've found
a catalpa grove to lie down and dream about lianas in,

if cicadas trill your family to sleep when the west
ocean moon cradles near. Are there cicadas there?

By now, I bet you've taught someone else to love the names
of everything: Foxtail Pine, Indian Mallow, Blazing

Star, Snowberry. Do you remember the poem I wrote
about my grandmother? She wore opals on her fingers

and turquoise bathrobes in the evenings and sang arias
when she made pot roast in her gold-linoleum kitchen.

I was thirteen when she told me that fucking
was a beautiful thing. You are the only one I know

who is as strange as she was. I'm not sure
she would have liked you. Two days ago, I was in a plane

for the first time in years, and I was scared until I saw
the sunset beneath me, deep indigo ahead, clouds

snaking like rivers in between. I could go on, but you told me
not to make poems out of sky. You told me that you don't

believe in gravity or hummingbirds, that roses don't belong
in notebooks, that I'm not yet as lovely as I could be.

Someday You'll Want This Too

I've spent all day in the woods
trying to picture myself with a swollen
belly, spent hours searching down side trails
for deer, imagining a smaller set of footprints
behind my own. My sister had a baby
seven days ago, and each night she croons
to me over the phone, *Just wait, you'll want this
someday, someday you'll want this too.* I've never
wanted a child, but I want desperately to find
a deer on this path, to let one stare at me
in its unflinching, dark, wild animal way,
for the space between us in the snow to grow
wide and significant. I wonder how many times
I've passed the place the deer bed down in,
how close I've come to catching the glow
of distant eyes. I've read that babies see
in black and white in their first weeks,
that my nephew's world is mostly out of focus
shadows, that if he met me now he'd see
only a patch of speaking, shifting light.
I have never thought babies were as lovely
as snow and everything beneath it—
vole nests and pine needles and dead ragweed,
years of dirt and stone buried in white—
but my sister says her son is *beautiful, so
beautiful.* His tiny hands and tiny fingers, tiny
mouth, tiny, faraway staring at his mother.

Raymond B. Winter State Park, Pennsylvania

1.

I have read

that there are owls

here,

     fairy shrimp

and caddisflies,

acres full

     of hidden eyes

and wings.

2.

Evergreens remind me
of funeral homes. Polished
pine and strange

embraces. I try not to write
about death, but maybe
all of my poems

are informed by memorial
services. My father
is a hunter. He shoots

deer and wild
turkey in the dead of winter,
spends hours in a tree

in Michigan, saying
nothing, hoping for a chance
to kill.

3.

This place
        is nothing like a city,

echo of moss
and lichen spore

        everywhere.

This place
        is so much like a city,

gray and broken
everywhere,

        underbrush full

of detached
        mandibles,

hollow exoskeleton
shine.

4.

I spend too much
of my time here
thinking about deer,
wondering if they
dream of summer
in mid-March,
if they
shrink away
at the sight
of spiders,
if they care
about finding
meaning
in the forest,
if they huddle
close together,
shaking
when it grows
cold at night,
if they hide
or run
when they hear me
on this path
drawing near.

5.

Everything is full
of the sound

      of winter leaving.

Sound of feather moss
returning
to forest floor,
sound of water bug,
sound of trees with branches
spindled toward sunlight
like spiders,

and sound of spiders
too.

Spiders hidden beneath
ages of dead leaves
and moth wings,

spiders
twining silk through
maple limbs,

spiders waiting
for fireflies
at twilight,

    spiders inching

toward the river
carefully.

6.

I wonder what my father
thinks of when he pulls
the trigger—maybe of the deer
and whether or not it will run, maybe

of the stillness in the trees
before violence.
Everything disappears
into hemlock here.

Trillium and black willow
obscured in needle-light,
whole bodies lost
to greenery. Today,

I found a bat facedown
beside the river, wings
becoming forest floor.

7.

Even the sky

        seems closer to me

when it's mirrored in water.

You Left,

and I ate all the sweet potatoes.
I'm sorry. The raspberries,
the honey, that locket

you gave me. They're gone.
I was so hungry. I ate
the metronome and the black

bear skull we keep on the bookshelf.
I ate the books. I ate the empty
frame on the wall. And our bed—

the mattress that was soaked
in rain when the roof leaked
mid-thunderstorm, the throw pillows,

the feathery down—I ate
it all. I was ravenous. I went outside.
Forgive me, but I ate

our lawn furniture. Even
the porch railings, covered in snow
and ice. I ate them whole.

I ate the neighbor's wind chimes.
I ate her welcome mat. Her dead
cactus. I went inside and watched

the sun filter into the living room
and light our couch up like an altar.
Then I ate it. The sunlight

and the couch. I was so hungry.
I left. I walked into town. I bought
a chicken from the market.

I brought it home and covered
it in butter. I roasted it.
I fried its kidneys in oil

and rosemary. I sautéed
its liver with shallots. I ate
its body slowly. I didn't

know what to do
with its heart. I sliced it into pieces.
I held them in my hands,

and they were red
against my skin. I baked
them into a pie.

It was a lovely thing. Golden
brown and bulging
at its seams. I didn't want

to eat it. It was beautiful,
but it tasted too much
like a chicken's heart. It tasted

like another body inside
my body. It tasted too much
like I had held it in my hands.

Letter for Anyone

I miss you most at night
and when the morning glories

close. The sky sounds like
an ocean here. At home,

like a highway. I haven't seen
a lily in this town, but every day

I watch the river stretching
toward its own end.

Maybe you will dream
about the mountain tonight.

Maybe black bear cubs
and caddisflies will swarm

around your bed. Listen:
the moon folds inward, slowly,
the rain cradles near us.

It's Sylvia's Birthday,

and already I've heard too many jokes
about *a woman who was no good
in the kitchen*. I think of her
when I look in the mirror, searching
for the terrible fish I know
is rising up to meet me.
I think of her when I light a candle
and wonder if she, like me
was always drawn to fire.
Even when I'm swooning
over her phrasing, I'm afraid of her.
Of the familiar lines in her face,
the talent for sadness, the extreme
ability to go to extremes. My heroines
are fierce and broken women.
Virginia too—her eyes wide
in photographs with some unknowable
question—reminds me too much
of someone I know too well.
A girl who collected stones
in her pockets for years
until she heard the story,
a girl who sometimes longs to touch
the black belly of the river.

Those Early Sunday Mornings

arced like sparrows diving into afternoon
and I sang to God in languages

I couldn't understand—*dante Deo, credo, credo*—
my mother raised her arms in praise.

I thought I loved a boy with red hair
and freckled wrists who took me into a basement

where the shelves brimmed with porcelain
angels--Mary standing in the center

like a searchlight--and knocked me down
onto his mattress, pressed his ribcage into mine,

found his way inside me, roughly.
I saw the virgin every night in my sleep

for six months after, her white palms open
in some vague gesture of condolence

or forgiveness. I left the church choir,
trying to forget her face, but still I heard

my mother mutter, *Deus, indulgeo nos.*
The red haired boy is married now. He spends

every night in the hollow of a different woman,
every day in a city skies away from me.

Sometimes I see a steeple and remember
his shelves full of angels, their pale,

closed lips and outstretched fingers, fury
of immobile wings.

He Misremembers

My cousins shot toy guns at cardinals
in the backyard while my sister and I

made shelters out of oak branches,
and grandpa scattered ears of corn

along the path into the forest,
because he wanted deer to wander

into the open, and he would call us
to the window to watch them skirt

around the well in the ground
that we were all afraid of falling into,

and grandma would play his favorite
song on the piano some nights,

and later, when she was gone,
he sometimes couldn't remember

our names, but he still walked
that path every night. He still spent

his evenings staring at the treeline,
waiting for something tender to emerge.

Personal History

There are stories I held close when I was young.
Princesses lost in golden towers, princesses awoken

by men crawling into their beds to touch them. At school, boys
chased girls and pinned us down on the playground,

pulled up our dresses and found white cotton beneath. Even then,
I knew to be ashamed. Later, when I told my best friend

what a boy with red hair did to me in his basement, she called me
whore. It was the Fourth of July. We were sixteen, lying on a dock

in bikinis our bodies had only just begun to fill. Blue and yellow
light streamed over our heads, the dark lake around us shining

as if it could catch fire at any moment. Both of us afraid
of being burned. Later still, when I had been touched

by too many men and needed to let some piece of myself go,
I asked the woman at the salon to take ten inches off.

Pretty girl, she said, *don't cut your hair*, but I was tired
of feeling like a woman.

Of Daves and Midwest Winters

My father is Dave, and his father
was Dave, and I was meant to be
Dave too, but my small body

betrayed the name. There is a photo
of the Daves I loved as a child:
two men surrounded by empty

pitchers of beer in the bar
they once owned, serious
faces and clenched hands

mirroring each other in tension,
a sameness I was almost
born into. I know a story

of a cold night in Michigan,
each Dave in a separate room
of a lakeside cabin. One

finishes a bottle of whiskey
and drives a tractor across
the frozen water. One

watches from his window
as the ice breaks, the tractor's
single beam of light illuminating

the winter beneath the glass.
Each Dave lives his whole
life separating himself

from the other. Years after
the tractor is gone, my father
makes my sister and me wait

in a snowbank while he walks
out onto a pond in mid-January.
He tests the ice with his weight,

leans down to inspect
the thickness of it
with gloveless fingers, careful

not to lose his daughters
to the water.

Detroit Riots, 1967

Mary, in white robes, is painted black,
arms outstretched as if to bless

the burning tenements and empty bar stools
of the blind pigs on Clairmont Avenue.

My grandfather sends his family forty miles south
and waits inside his door with rifle pointed.

Every department store window
on Lafayette is spiderwebbed, mannequin

limbs and crinoline skirts are strewn across concrete
like the city is exploding, storefront

by storefront. *A man's got to protect*
his own, grandfather says

as smoke gouges the sky in the distance.
Night comes and the streets are wrapped

in flame. Men step on downed power lines
and fall, bone marrow transformed

into aluminum light. *I will take on any boy*
who knocks on this door, grandfather says,

and he will fall asleep like this—
slumped over in the hall with a gun

on his shoulder, waiting for the sound
of voices outside, glass shattering

in the next room, anything
he can shoot at.

Poem for Jillian Michaels

I find your videos on the internet,
and my body begins
the strange process of addition
and subtraction. You say,
kick harder, and I kick

harder. You make a fist,
and I make one too. I lose
myself in shapes I never knew
my limbs could make. Jillian,
I have been told so many times

that I am small. I practice violence
in the mirror every morning.
I watch myself cross-jab,
uppercut. I try to move faster,
cleaner, better, more

like you. My mother is worried
about me, but she shouldn't be.
How do I explain it, Jillian?
I don't want less of myself,
just more

of what's strong. I think of you
when I walk down the street
alone. Men look at me,
and I want them to see
a weapon. Jillian,

I want them to be afraid.
You sweat as you lunge
toward me, and you say, *You
can do this. You're not gonna
die*, and you're wrong.

We are both going to die,
Jillian, both of us will quit
when we're old or broken,
but I promise you, Jillian,
I promise we will never
be small.

Doe, Meadow, Moonlight

Any other day, dad is a hunter, but for now he only wants
to show us fields full of deer, tall grass populated

with brown eyes and bowed heads. We drive toward
Little Bay de Noc, a name I thought meant *little bay*

of night when I was small. The deer come slowly
and then all at once. A fawn kneels beside a whirligig

in someone's garden. A buck, *six points*, dad says,
lifts its head up from the browse line. We reach

a clearing, and at least thirty deer stare back at us,
some lounging on the ground, some hiding behind

wildflowers, all aware of being watched. I try
to take a picture, but they are too fast for me.

Too much distance between their fear
and my finger on the trigger. We drive back

to the cabin, the bay's dark water churning
to our left. I know now that it's named

for the Noquet, a tribe that lived along its shores
until it couldn't. We see a doe alone

in a meadow. She is unafraid of us.
She stands still enough for me to photograph her,

still enough for me to open the door
of the truck and come closer. Her head tilts up

like she's looking at the moon. I want her
to stay there forever, perfect in that blue

light. I want her to run. To disappear
in cedar. I want her to know
when she's being targeted.

I Remember the Field

behind the old house
and the bright days spent
running through it, grass

so sharp we cut our hands.
There were things they kept hidden
from us. The hatchet rusting

in the shed and the well
in the woods behind
the field, mouth covered

in cattails and Queen Anne's lace.
There were things they wanted
to save us from

and couldn't. We all fell
from the oak in the yard
and broke our bones,

we all watched our aunt
lose her breasts and waste
away. We found more

in the field than we wanted
to find. A whole family
of rabbits killed

in a flood, a robin's wing
torn away from its body,
and a bullet

that we took turns
carrying in our pockets
like a talisman,

not knowing what it was
or where it had been.

Upon Watching the Murder of
Another Woman in a Crime Scene Drama,

I am amazed at how lovely
a corpse can be made
to look. Slight arc

of the neck, of the arms.
How the hands, purple now, curl
just so, how the toes

point as if she might
begin to dance. Precision
in the woman

cut down. I think
of Emily, killed months ago
in a subway tunnel,

left whole somehow
by passing trains.
It was twelve hours

before anyone noticed her
beneath the tracks, so small
she could have been

mistaken for an animal
that got in someone's way.

Aubade in a Railyard

I think of my love
in terms of crabgrass

and whiskey
and Lake Michigan.

When I stroke
his broken chest,

he makes a sound
like a crow sighing.

Remember, I say,
I have written

a thousand poems
to your kneecaps.

He draws for me
an astrolabe,

and I weigh
its shadow

in dried lavender
and steel.

Catcall #27

Slow down baby, slow down baby, you look so good from behind, baby slow down, please slow down baby, damn, he said, and I slowed down. I slowed all the way down. I lay down there in the street. I stayed still so he could see all of me in the way he wanted to see it. *Damn baby,* he said, and he took me in his arms. *Damn baby,* he said, and he kissed me just to see what I felt like. He traced the outline of my legs. He found the shape of what he owned. *Damn baby,* he said, and he married me right there. He made children with me. I stayed still. *Damn baby,* he said. Our daughters filled the street. Their legs, their mouths, their gentle hands. They grew tall. I watched them walk away from me. They watched me watch them walk away. Their father watched us watching each other, all of us learning what our bodies can do.

In Flight

Clouds stretch out in white rows
for miles beside the plane, a whole

orchard of sky and milky gleaming.
I think of what you told me

about Missouri, of the wheat fields
and their swaying glow,

the girl you used to dream about
with blond hair and skinny knees

and too much faith in what
she couldn't touch. I can never

explain the Great Lakes to people
who haven't seen them.

The vastness. The exact shade of blue.
Even now, above Lake Michigan,

I can't find the end of it, the shore
below me. I imagine seagulls

circling somewhere in the space
between cloud and water,

whole lives lived in descent
and in flight. Turbulence

on the plane, and I think
of my grandmother bent over

her third glass of cabernet, years
buried in the same quiet town.

You've never asked about my past.
The nights spent in unlit

basements, the boys who thought
their bodies were gifts to be unwrapped,

stories I am happy not to tell you.
The plane bends in toward Chicago,

and I am trying not to grip
the arms of my seat too tightly,

trying not to show that I'm afraid
of losing the sky

I've grown used to having
beneath me.

How to Leave Home

1.

The key is to open
like zinnias into June's undoing.

Learn to be enchanted
with rain and the ivy

it sends curling
toward your window.

Let your hair grow long.
Plant a garden and lie down

in lemon balm, breathe in cilantro,
count spines of rosemary

until evening and its crickets
crowd you out.

2.

Thunder like the waves
of Lake Michigan

will creep into your dreams some nights.
Pretend the sound you hear

is a car alarm. A sparrow's call. A drunk
in the alley at 3 AM. Freight train

howl. River water. Anything
but the thing you miss most.

3.

Forget the lakeside dunes,
the water-smoothed stones

you've left behind.
Entwine yourself in morning

and its bare-skinned
ringing. Think lip of iris,

dogwood blossom,
marigold. Things

that close.

The Weight of Lumens

Light exerts force on matter,
          says the voice in the documentary,
and I think of photons pushing river water
          deeper into its channel,
photons spiraling golden over my head
          the first week of July every year,
photons making me want to reach
          up and touch their shining.
Light = photon x frequency,
          and I think there must be
an equation too
          for the safety I find in photons
silvering the night around me
          when I walk alone at 2 AM,
photons raining out of cloudless
          sky into creek bed, photons
huddling in the moon
          of a streetlamp. There is a comfort
in heaviness born of lumens,
          consistency in stars
careening gaseous brightness
          into gaseous brightness.
I have trouble in the absence
          of photons, difficulty sleeping
without gleaming making shards
          of darkness all around me.
I imagine photons hung
          in streams around my room
like banners, photons wrapped

around my limbs
like planetary jewelry.
      I am grateful to the makers
of photons--milky halos of galaxies
      miles and miles out of sight
still in sight, supernovas full
      of hydrogen turning away
from itself, cosmic fireflies
      that leave a trail of neon even
at their ending.

For Ruby

Somewhere in Michigan,
my grandmother is dying. I'm learning
to sew again. I pull the thread
through the needle's eye and begin
to bring two pieces of cloth together.
You don't have to come home,
my sister said. My stitching is loopy
and uneven. *She's already gone.* I don't need
to make a pretty thing, I only need
to close an opening.
My grandmother was not
a woman who sewed. She was a woman
of tiny porcelain birds. Birds
of glass. Birds painted red
and blue. They lined the shelves
of her apartment. Everything
in that place ready to fly.
Even a cherry branch carved
with the likeness of a hummingbird.
And a picture on the wall
that my sister and I colored
as children: three larks in a meadow,
the sky behind them golden
like we thought we could draw
something holy. I hold my first
row of stitches up to the light.
I don't know what I'm making,

but I know I want to give it form
and weight. I want to fill it
with something clean. I want
to keep it close to me.

The Trouble with Love

Yes, I am afraid of our bodies.
Afraid you will become the man I knew

in Pennsylvania. The one who went
to the doctor and learned his intestines

were lined with tumors, that the cancer
would spread and bloom within him.

How his wife must have touched him
with shaking hands. How their daughter

must have wanted to curl up beside him
when he lay sick in bed. To ask him

to read her a story. When I tell you this,
you sigh and kiss the crown of my head.

We spend the afternoon reading
on the couch. The dog asleep

in the corner. Apartment shot with light.
Our bodies close. Our bodies quiet

and heavy. Each of us just beginning to know
the danger in holding the other.

Toward Center

Something about travel
makes us lighter. We drive
to Missouri, and I discover

prairies. There is space
for doubt in the Northern plains.
Space for undoing. When I say

expansion, this is what I mean:
Iowa, full of grain silos
and white houses. Iowa,

wide and unmoving. We are lost
somewhere near Des Moines,
and everything

is cornfields and yellow flowers
in highway medians. Wherever
we are going, it is golden.

Catcall #86

There is a man on the street
coming toward you. He walks the way
you imagine a fly might walk if it stood upright.
Like his body is lighter than he expects
it to be. Like part of him is missing.
He howls something strange
and unintelligible. Maybe he's calling
for you. Maybe he wants to touch you.
To hurt you. Maybe he's just keening
like an old cat. You wonder
if you should run. If you should
take refuge in the little convenience store
on the corner. The one with chocolates
wrapped in gold paper. With the cashier
who smiles at you and says *hello,*
sweetie in a voice so heavy
you can barely understand it
when you are tired. You wonder
if you should yell for help. If you
should hide. But you stand there
and watch him draw nearer,
snow arranging itself in soft walls
on the sidewalk. A better woman
would walk away. A better woman
would know what to do
when a man is coming for her
in the dark.

A Brief Imagined Disaster

The plane goes down somewhere over Iowa. Crashes in farmland, the smoke visible for miles and miles. No secrets in the wheat fields. People pull off the highway to stare at the wreck. *Prairie fire*, someone jokes. No one laughs. No one knows what they are looking at. The plane a twisted thing in the dirt. I'm at work when I find out he is dead. *Flight 93 goes down in Iowa*, the headline says. *No bodies in the amber waves. No bodies in the flat expanse.* I remember his body pressed into mine in the shower the day before he left. *Don't forget to feed the dog*, he said. I walk home, and it snows in a way that can't be real. The city cold and rushing. I remember that it was once a prairie too. Bluestem grass along the streets. Horizon in place of steel. The river wider, hungrier, eroding the land. In our apartment, the dog leaps all over me in happiness. She has missed me all day. Has wanted just the scent of me. We lie on the couch together. We both need the warmth of the other, need to curl up next to something whole.

Three Girls in a Field

All day they've called each other names, stripped petals off daisies pulled up from the dirt. Now they chase each other. Now they sing to each other across the field. Sing *ruby lips above the water.* Sing *oh, my darling.* Sing *dreadful sorry.* There is a hole in the ground near a patch of carrot flowers, its opening covered in dead oak branches. They skirt around it. Sing *you are lost and gone forever.* At home, they wash their hands. They eat supper. They crawl into bed and dream about the field. About the hole and what is buried in it. They get older. One girl moves south. She lives near a swamp with a man she doesn't love. She paints landscapes and drinks too much gin, humming as she renders algae over water. Some nights, when she has had enough, she tells stories about the girls in the field. How they whispered to each other as they searched for thistle. How they ate dandelions when they were hungry. How their mouths turned yellow. How they ran. One girl dies early. Crushed in a truck on a highway at night. *Such a shame,* says everyone at her funeral, shuffling past her closed casket. She didn't like heights. When the other girls climbed the oak in the middle of the field, she waited on the ground, listening as they dared each other higher. Sometimes she cried when they left her there. Sometimes they teased her from above. Sang *cry baby, cry baby.* Sang *poor little baby, run home to your mother.* The last girl works midnight shifts at a gas station mini-mart. She likes the order of the shelves, of the cash register, the smooth counter. She likes leaving at 4 AM and knowing she's alone in the dark. She is never far from the field. She thinks of it sometimes when there are lulls at the shop, when the customers have gone and there is nothing left to clean or sort. She remembers dancing wild in the field with the other girls, scaring rabbits away. She remembers hiding under the big oak during a thunderstorm, shaking in the rain. She remembers the stone they buried near the carrot flowers. How they gasped when they found it in the tall grass. How they laughed and passed it bashfully to one another, the naked woman painted on its surface sad and strange-looking. Her body poised like a shotgun. How they traced the shapes of her breasts with their fingers. How they wanted both to hold her in their hands and to be rid of her forever, all of them scared of what they might become.

How to Write a Poem about Anxiety

Stop. Already, you worry that the first line
is no good. See how the child on the sidewalk
laughs as his sister pulls him in her wagon,
happy in the act of letting go. See the pigeons
in straight lines on your rooftop, the strange
geometry of wings not-flying. See how the city,
cloaked in rain, still gleams—sidewalks lit
with broken glass, river cleaving through
the center of it all, searching for its mouth.
See the bees at work in your neighbor's garden
in spite of what you've heard on the news,
teaching you persistence, teaching you
not to disappear.

Parenthetical

Somewhere in Illinois,
a woman buries every poem
that breaks her heart.

I plant bone meal
in the garden. I plant sugar.
I forget everything

I have tried to destroy—
the Midwest sky
in my memory like

an open vein
and you painting watercolors
on the beach, a kind

of flight. How often
we make projects of each other.
I lose mountain ranges

in search of you, tributaries
full of amber light. I watch
hemlock forests

disappear. We give up
whole futures for each other
again and again.

My love, I am grateful
for what I've thrown away.

Acknowledgments

The author is grateful to the editors of the publications in which the following poems first appeared:

Apercus Quarterly: "The Weight of Lumens"

Atticus Review: "It's Sylvia's Birthday," "Of Daves and Midwest Winters," "Catcall #86," "For Ruby," "How to Go Home," "In Flight," and "Upon Watching the Murder of Another Woman in a Crime Scene Drama"

Bird's Thumb: "Poem for Jillian Michaels" and "Raymond B. Winter State Park, Pennsylvania"

Bodega: "Catcall #48"

Columbia College Literary Review: "Letter for M"

Corium Magazine: "How to Leave Home" and "Someday You'll Want This Too"

Lunch Ticket: "You Left"

Prick of the Spindle: "He Misremembers" and "Parenthetical"

Split Lip Magazine: "Letter for Anyone" and "Toward Center"

Watershed Review: "Catcall #27"

Michelle S. Reed is a poet, embroi-
derer, and teacher. She grew up in
Michigan. *I Don't Need to Make a
Pretty Thing* is her first full-length
collection.